MW00763495

Waking
in the Dark

For Kathleen,
With Good Wishes
Michael Miller
Dec 7, 2019

Also by
Michael Miller

The Joyful Dark
The Singing Inside
Darkening the Grass
Into This World
Lifelines
The Different War
In the Mirror
Asking the Names

WAKING

IN THE DARK

POEMS BY

MICHAEL MILLER

PINYON PUBLISHING

Montrose, Colorado

Copyright © 2019 by Michael Miller

All rights reserved. Except as permitted under the U.S. Copyright Act of 1976, no part of this publication may be reproduced, distributed, or transmitted in any form or by any means, or stored in a database or retrieval system, without the prior written permission of the publisher, except for brief quotations in articles, books, and reviews.

Cover Art by Susan Entsminger

Photograph of Michael Miller by Mary Miller

First Edition: March 2019

Pinyon Publishing
23847 V66 Trail, Montrose, CO 81403
www.pinyon-publishing.com

Library of Congress Control Number: 2019930188
ISBN: 978-1-936671-54-0

ACKNOWLEDGMENTS

Some of these poems, in slightly different versions, appeared in:

Connecticut River Review
Hanging Loose
Mudfish
Passager
Pinyon Review
Poetry Daily on line
Raritan

For Harlon

CONTENTS

I

II

III

IV

These are the days when birds come back,
A very few, a bird or two,
To take a backward look.

—Emily Dickinson

I

SLEEVE

In the rear-view mirror
They vanish, the maples
With ice-coated branches
Drawing me back to the magicians
Of childhood who made things
Appear, disappear,
Their top hats and wands
Vivid in the long mirror
Of memory. Innocence still
Lives inside me, silent as
The space between dreams,
Waiting to be pulled out
Of a sleeve, its white wings
Fluttering into the air.

TRACES OF JOANNA

Lying on my side,
Facing the window
And the early light,
I imagine Joanna,
Her arm around my waist
Never wanting to let go,
Her fourteenth spring
Refusing to be her last,
Rampaging disease
Vanishing from her blood,
Her life no longer
A pale blossom
Wilted by May's end,
Its petals falling with
Unbearable silence.
Cut off from possibilities,
The future no longer a dream,
Death removed its disguises
To embrace Joanna,
But I embrace her with
Unspoken love,
Looking for traces of Joanna
In every woman's face.

POINTS OF REFERENCE

On Sunday mornings
I climbed into her warm bed,
Not making a sound.
Turning away, Mother left me
Her exposed back,
Allowing me to count
The moles I wanted to touch,
This map of beauty
With points of reference
I would seek in each woman
I began to love.

THE RING

In the long minutes of a dream fading
My head nods to the man above me
Who had run across
The black sand of Iwo Jima;
I see his Catholic hand strike my face
After every new sin
When his clear words failed again.
Almost my father he became my father
With his hard love, his stinging beliefs
Reddening my cheek.
Following his footsteps, I joined
The Marines. I wanted the medals
Of blood he kept in a box.
But there was no war then,
My war continued with him for years,
Ending when I came to his deathbed.
Now I wear his sapphire ring;
I never kissed him—I kiss the ring.

CADENCE

The sunset bruise in the distance
Spread across the stark Mojave
As I walked away from the rattlesnake
Coiled on a rock, wishing I could
Leave the Marine Corps, never return
To my rifle, the drilled marching,
The training for war.
Esprit de corps had worn off;
My tattoo, a visible stigma,
Remained, the snake around
The dagger on my forearm.
On liberty I wore long sleeves,
Never mentioned the Marines
To the women I met.
Love came slowly, a different
Cadence resounding within.

EMILY'S ANGELS

On a cold morning
With no bird in sight
She tells me quietly
To return to my warm house.
Once again I listen,
Sitting on the weathered bench
By her house that faces
The bare oak,
The white garden,
The snow falling
Like the ashes of burnt angels,
Emily's angels
With invisible wings
Lifting the soul
In the silence of love
After barbed words.
Through each season I have
Walked the mile to her house
To contemplate the great oak,
Dwell upon the garden
And seek solace.
Age has not brought wisdom
Nor the acceptance
Of the flaws in marriage.
"You should return," Emily says
And rises from the bench
To walk through the snow,
Her arm extended,
Her hand opened.

DIVERGENCE

Each morning I imitate
Your smile in the mirror,
Beginning the day
More close to you,
Knowing how quickly
We can argue, draw apart,
One more divergence
In our old age,
As if this were
The wrong turning of love
And not our quiet dread
Of that final separation.

SEVEN IN THE MORNING

Mist blurs the sugar maples
As I walk toward them,
Trusting the mist will lift,
The sun appear,
And my eyes with moons
Of cataracts will see better.
Reality draws me
Closer to diminishment,
My sibling in old age.
Even your loveliness
Cannot change things.
With my fountain pen
I draw a feather for you.
I might never see
A bluebird again.

AT MIDNIGHT

Floating on the pond
Surrounded by pines
The full moon seemed like a hole
I could swim through
With nothing holding me back,
Leaving you to swim freely.

Then you called, waving from
The water's edge, taking off
Your clothes, your whiteness
One with the moon,
Your breasts nameless twins
As I swam toward you.

IN THE SENSUAL DARK

With my back to the wall
Her naked body
Pressed against mine
As I awakened
In the sensual dark
Folding into yesterday.
I dwelt upon
This uninvited guest
Closer than you
In the suburb of dreams.
I wanted to carry this dream
Through the day, into the night,
But it was fading over
My coffee and the obituaries.
I could only retrieve
The white wall
She pressed me against
In a room with no window,
No door, as her face
Fit perfectly between
My shoulder and neck.
Half my life has been driven
To seek the perfect fit:
The right words
In the right place,
My starlings flying
Without a comma between them,
The perfect sex with you.

We say love has bound us
But lust keeps me alive
Through days and dreams
In my seventy-seventh winter,
Old fires burning anew.

THE SPACE

Your hand is always first
To leave, to draw away
After making love.
Separateness becomes you
As beauty becomes
The blue iris unfolding
In a corner of your garden.
Once I hoped to change you,
Now love grows stronger
In the wide space we share.

IN THE DISTANCE

When I chance upon you
Looking at the display
Of blouses in the store window
I am instantly entranced,
Falling in love again,
Knowing how love
Renews itself
Through the eye,
Through the heart.

MADNESS IN THE MORNING

I hurried, hurried toward
The high-pitched cries—
An animal in a trap?
It was Ruth, kneeling before
The leather couch in the lobby,
Staring into the eyes
Of her small, trembling dog
And screaming, "If you die I die!";
To me, "Keep away, get the police,
My house is burning,
I'll torch the whole building!"
Riveted to the moment
I said, "Wait here, I'll call."
Ten minutes later,
Wheeled out on a gurney
She screamed, "My dog, my Pluto!"
And her dog ran back and forth
Sniffing the floor, the elevator door
Until I held it in my arms,
Something inside me breaking.

ALIVE

After our son walked away from
A high-speed crash
As the sun rose over the bayous
On the first day of his fishing trip
I prayed silently.
In the dusk of unknowing
Belief is personal, faith optional.
Our son is miraculously alive,
Hugging his children fiercely.

OUT OF RUINS

Who will sing in Syria,
Lament the death in spring?
A hand juts out of ruins,
A child rots under rubble.
What flowers grow in Syria?—
The forever blossoms
Cut for a bouquet of death.

BY THE POND

Not from the small rectangular box
But from your hand
Will my ashes be scattered
Among the weeds and cattails
Surrounding the pond
Where we walked at dusk
To see the great blue heron
Wade into the water to stalk
The carp wriggling like flame.
If I am destined to live longer
I will take the handfuls of you
And offer them to the grass
By this spring-fed pond
Where you swam in summer,
Where our son caught his first fish.
Months or years later
He will spread my ashes;
The flakes and chips of bone
Falling from his hand that
Once fit so perfectly into mine.

II

GUIDES

A man with no agenda
Pays little attention
To the clock on the dresser.
But the sun lifting over the hill,
The thrush singing on
A sumac branch
Become his guides
To welcome each new day.
If death arrives in
An hour or ten years
He hopes to be surprised,
Like the red fox appearing
At the fork in the road,
Its left foreleg raised,
A blaze of indecision.

SEEING

He cleans his glasses and continues
Toward the sugar maples, the oaks.
His need is to see clearly,
To understand his wife's
Infidelity, to determine
If he can live with it.

He observes the small ridges
In the long pink worm
Inching across the grass,
He notices the differences
Between the birds in the trees,
The wren from the sparrow,
The goldfinch from the yellow warbler,
Then marvels at the differences.

Emerson accepted all,
Loving through ambivalence,
Never acknowledging Thoreau's
Attraction to his wife,
His penetrating vision
Seeing into his friend's heart,
The tangles of need,
The silent desperation.

CURSIVE

Last night, in an old woman's
Cursive she made a list of memories
From the day she met Hannah.
When she visits each week
Hannah will be sitting
By the window facing the pond
In the blue solarium.
In that hour, an addition
To their decades in Berlin
And Vienna, she will speak with
The tenderness inside a rose,
Finding a part of fulfillment
Despite the veils of sorrow:
Hannah, her gaze fixed upon
The algaed pond,
May understand something
Of what she is saying
As sunlight falls on
Half her face.

PARIS MORNING

He remembered that gray
Paris morning, the statues
With empty eyes looking down
In the Tuileries.
She said they had seen
So much pain,
Had wept for so long
Their pupils were washed away.

A MAN ALONE

Eating his muffin
And drinking his coffee
He swallows his fear of death,
Breakfasting with the obituaries,
Glimpsing into the lives
Of strangers,
Imagining which man,
Which woman, might have
Joined him for dinner.

CONCERT

Before the music,
In the long silence
Of the moment,
A powerful attraction
Draws him to the woman
With an empty seat beside her—
The closeness as real
As Schubert's first notes.
How swiftly imagination
Leads him to take her face,
Kiss her slowly,
A blue-eyed gray-haired woman
With sculpted features,
Sorrow inside her wrinkles.
If he ever says hello
He will never leave her,
Never return to the life
He has built
After his wounds,
His marriage.

6:00 A.M.

He raises a slat of the blind,
Peers through the space;
He has always been drawn
To small spaces:
The cracks in the sidewalk
Where the weeds grow.
Now he sees a skunk
Crossing the wet grass,
Its stripe a pathway
Of light dividing the dark.
Opening the blind
He enters the day—
Treasures are waiting
To be discovered,
He must keep on looking.

A THIN BRANCH

First his wife, then his firstborn,
His willowy daughter wasting away
In her forty-fifth spring,
Two deaths in two years
And now his seventy-fifth birthday
When the cherry tree blooms.
He raises his face to
A thin branch crowded with
Pink and white blossoms,
Inhales the sweetness
That has gone out of him,
This fragile beauty
A sudden storm will sweep away.

IN RIVERSIDE PARK

Dreaming of a magnolia blossom unfolding
He opens his bloodshot eyes,
Waking in the dark
On a bench in Riverside Park,
The coins in his frayed pocket
Clinking against a half-empty bottle.

Rising slowly, he walks
To the promenade railing
And looks down at
The swirling Hudson;
Sudden dizziness offers him
A glimpse of his death.

"I'm alive," he says,
Spreading his arms
Tattooed with roses and daggers,
Opening his mouth to
Gulp down the dark,
Assured the sky will lighten.

CONFESSION

He was trained to kill the enemy;
Women and children were killed by mistake.
He kept a bible in his pocket,
Touched it before each mission.
In the priestly dirt
He made his quiet confession,
Saying again and again
He had no choice.

MESSENGERS

When two Marines walked toward
Her house she turned from
The living room window
And knew her husband was dead.
She braced herself against the table
As the doorbell chimed,
A bomb exploding inside her.

SOLDIER DREAMING

He dreams of a bullet
Ricocheting off the Humvee
And piercing his lung.
He dreams of a Taliban
In bed with his wife
Wearing his dog tags.

THE LAST STRAWBERRIES

Leaving his dream behind
He turns onto his side,
Moves his feet to the floor
And sits up slowly,
Gazing at his old man's legs,
The muscles in his calves
Diminished through the years.
Pressing his fists against
The mattress he rises,
A thin tower of bone.
"Good morning," he says,
Making sure his voice
Is still there.
Now there is oatmeal to prepare,
The last strawberries
To place on top.
He whispers the word
He loves, the word delicious,
To the strawberries waiting.

NAMING STRANGERS

With no one in her life
To call a friend
She names the strangers
In her dreams, an old woman
On the forgotten side of spring.
In her room growing smaller
Each year, the newspapers
Are stacked beside her bed.
"I'm living my obituary,"
She thinks, walking in the park
Every morning, and to the birds
At the fountain she calls out:
"Blue, Tiny, Beak."

THE WOMAN IN
THE LIBRARY

Trying to return to sleep
He imagines the woman
In the library beside him.
He has never asked her name
But has memorized her smile,
A woman in the shade of fifty
Without a wedding ring.
He would like to learn
About her life, to let her
Become a part of his own,
His old age lost in her presence.

HOPE

He rises, sits on the edge
Of his bed and arranges
His sparse hair with his hands,
Not wanting to look in the mirror
At his red eyes,
A man at the wrong end
Of his years beginning his day
With the hope of seeing
The black-capped chickadee.
It was there yesterday,
On the sycamore branch
Behind his house,
Its small being his large joy.

ANOTHER SPRING

The old gardener often dreams
Of purple irises
But tonight she cannot sleep.
Within arm's reach
The bedside lamp shines;
She imagines the sun
Warming her face.
"Another spring," she thinks,
Remembering her lush garden,
The pleasure of planting.
She wishes the leftover rags
Of snow would melt.
She turns off the lamp,
Dwelling on the green tips
Of crocuses emerging—
Soon the blossoms will come.

ACROSS THE HALL

Now his speech was slow,
Garbled, his words lagging behind
His thoughts, so he wrote letters
To the woman across the hall,
A sister of kindness
Who always said good morning.
With a smile he replied,
Tilting to his right as if
He were leaning on the wind,
A tall man walking
With a new desire.
One day he will give her the letters.

JUBILANT

His bones, picked clean,
Were left to chance
When unknown hands lifted
His coffin lid.
He awakened, throwing back
The blanket as he rose quickly,
Set his feet firmly
And began to dance,
Old but jubilant
With arms opened wide.

III

HALF-MAD WOMAN

I

She spoke softly,
Told the willow
She would be silent until
She talked to it tomorrow,
Her hair like twigs
Twisted into the sunlit air.
She reached for a tassel,
Moved her hand
Along its length,
Whispered something
Inscribed in her dreams,
Let it go with
The gentleness
She remembered,
A half-mad woman
Offering her love.

II

Touching the beard of moss
On the rock, she imagined
Her father's whiskers,
How she wanted
To nest inside them,
To never come out.
After he shaved she felt
The coldness of bone,
The hardness
Beneath the surface.

III

On the overgrown path
To the pond she called back
To the loon,
Walking briskly to see
The glossy black head
And neck with a white collar.
"Loon, loon," she hurried,
Its beauty driving her blood.

IV

Through their ramshackle house
Her mother had chased her,
Raised the broom,
Screamed she would sweep her
Out the door
And feed her to the bears.
But she loved the bears,
They would circle round her,
Protect her.

V

"I'm not crazy, not crazy,"
She muttered as she
Strode across the meadow
And moved through
The doorway of leaves,
Entrance into the woods.
"Stupid boys, moron boys,"
And she pushed aside
Their mean words to imagine
The deer or the fox
She would see.

VI

The woman in her dreams,
Robust through the years,
Always offered her
A hot meal, and she ate
The ample portion, leaving
Something for the finches.
In her sketchbook she drew
The woman's face, returning
To it when she needed
Someone to talk to,
Someone who would
Never turn away.

IV

SUNRISE AT THE FOUNTAIN

The white-bearded man
Washed the night from his face
At the fountain, his shopping bags
Bulging as he lifted them
With his huge arms
And walked toward the woods;
He reminded me of Whitman,
His full-bodied beard
Bristling in the wind,
The brim of his hat turned up.
I could have followed him,
Catching up to him
On the pine-needled trail
To ask, "Tell me about the love
That reaches out to multitudes."
Then the beeping of a truck
Backing into a driveway—
The sparrows disappeared
With my imaginings.
I should have given him money,
He would have taken it
Like Walt with a smile.

RESURRECTION,
SAID THE CROW

Yesterday a limping crow,
Robber and scavenger,
Surveyed the field
I cross each morning.
In the indifferent air
We walked together,
Two pallbearers with
An invisible coffin between us.
I stopped, the crow stopped.
I knelt and waited;
A buried love rose
From a place inside me.
Neither of us moved,
A glossy crow with
A continual hunger,
An old man with no food
Welcoming the sunlight.
Slowly I opened my arms,
Imagined this damaged bird
Coming into them,
Nesting against my chest.

WINGS

Those perfect early mornings
When we lived near
The wildlife sanctuary
Return with the beating
Of large wings,
The great white heron
Dividing the sky,
Its underside illuminated
By sunrise, its long
Curving neck craning
Into the clear light.
To begin those days
With grace so apparent
Lifted me out of the darkness
On those wide white wings.

ONE PATH

First my shirt, then trousers,
Shoes and underwear
And I begin to live,
Walking naked through
The sweet smelling summer woods,
Passing pink pouches
Of lady's-slippers
Ridged like my old scrotum.
With only one path to follow,
Stripped of choices,
Of decades of camouflage:
The lies to spare the feelings
Of others, the anger controlled,
The need to break free let loose,
I am one with the bear
Ambling with grace in each step,
The deer nibbling the leaves.
I see a black-masked bandit
Waddling across the trail toward
A darker part of the woods.
I will stay on my own path.

ACREAGE

On a certain day in late autumn,
After leaving my faults and regrets
On the acreage of sleep,
I could swallow the sun,
The finches serenading each other
On the telephone wire,
The sugar maple's red leaves
And the needles beneath the tower
Of pine with drooping branches.
This is my preparation
For the New England winter,
My storehouse with portions
Of everything I love
With you the conclusion,
Woman of warmth
Opening your eyes
As my lips greet your shoulder
And you rise with the abundance
That has nurtured me
Through the blur of years.
It was never about
The locking of thighs
On that passionate ride
Where we fit perfectly together.
It was always about intimacy,
The understanding embrace,
The tenderness coming out
Of the dark that lifted us
With invisible hands.

LANDING

Smiling broadly, declaring your presence
As you entered the house, you shook
The snow off your hair and described
The eagle, spreading your arms to show
How it landed on the weather vane
Of Town Hall. White hooded, yellow beaked,
I unfolded my wings and flew toward you,
Looked out over the fields, the houses
Ascending the hills. We have never
Forgotten the bald eagle on the field,
A bullet hole clean through its breast.

IN SLEEP MY HAND
FINDS ITS WAY

In sleep my hand finds its way
Toward yours, fingers touching,
Palm over palm with the space
Between for love's place,
Love remaining intact,
Love unshaken by anger,
By words never forgotten,
Words slowly forgiven.

WEALTH

We lay on that field,
A yellow quilt of dandelions
Vibrant in the midday sun,
And nothing in the world,
Nothing in our minds disturbed us.
I knew then this was perfection
Never to be chanced on again.
We cannot remember the location
Of that field in New Hampshire
Nor the road that led us there—
How golden we felt,
How enormous the yellow wealth.

MAKING LOVE IN PITTSBURGH

In a hotel room with a wide window
That looked onto three rivers,
An abandoned mill, a brick church
With a cross glowing through the night
We made silent passionate love.
The brightness from that cross fell
Upon our bodies, lifted our spirits
Until we transcended lust and rose into
A numinous realm where the past and a place
Became one—it was derelict Pittsburgh in its
Glory, it was men forging steel in behemoth
Furnaces, it was the soul longing for
Tenderness as strong as iron, as bridges.

DECADES AGO

Shoveling the snow
As if I were shoveling
Death away, my gloved hands
Gripping the handle firmly,
I clear the driveway
Bordered by tall pines,
Bending, lifting,
An old man young with desire,
Thinking of the woman
I met decades ago
Who waits in the house.

THE HEARTBEAT WITHIN

The whispers began
In the realm of a dream,
In the grip of passion
Elusive for months;
Slow down, be patient,
Time is the heartbeat within.

Your richness covered my body,
No longer an old man's
But driven by fire
That bound us once
Through winters, through summers,
In beds where soul became body.

My eyes opened,
I rose with brittle bones
And walked with
Careful steps,
Leaving you to your dream,
Holding mine close.

MORTAR

How natural was our free-fall
Into love, surrendering
The need to control.

It has taken time
To hear each other's thoughts,
To enter each other's dreams.

Rather than diminishing us
The years have nurtured us
Without our knowledge.

More than body against body
Words have drawn us closer,
Language the mortar that binds.

CPSIA information can be obtained
at www.ICGtesting.com
Printed in the USA
FSHW012306100319
56189FS